Don't Ask

If You Don't Want To Know

10 Surefire Ways to Clean Up Your Messy Life

Jeanie Frankavitz

Do you want to know how to be the best you can be?

Do you want to know how to raise great children?

Do you want to know how to have a great work life?

Do you want to have a great marriage?

Well, *Don't Ask If You Don't Want To Know*!

DEDICATION

To Russell, Caitlin, Philip, Michael and Aiyana. I thought I knew what life was all about until I saw it come full circle through your eyes. May you always know what great love and happiness you have brought your Gimah. Thank you for being my inspiration.

RAVING REVIEWS

"Packed With Practical Advice And Sassy Wit!"

"Jeanie Frankavitz does a fantastic job anticipating exactly what you'll need to implement her *10 Surefire Ways to Clean Up Your Messy Life*. Her straight-shooting book, *Don't Ask If You Don't Want to Know*, is packed with practical advice and sassy wit on how to improve your life and build healthy relationships with everyone in your life. This was a clearly thought out product made with love and I loved every bit of it." --Lena Anani, Author of *OMG Do It Now: Be the Voice You Want to Hear in the World*

"I Can Use All Of The Advice Given!"

"Jeanie Frankavitz, author of *Don't Ask if You Don't Want to Know* does an amazing job expressing her views on becoming the best you can be in your work and family life. Frankavitz's authentic joyful personality is seen through her storytelling and positive outlook on life. Although I am not a mother myself, I feel that I can use all of the advice given to raise and teach my future children (or anyone) to become good responsible people, which will make the world a better place!" --Crystal Simpelo, Author of *The Colorful Expressions of Your Soul*, CrystalSimpelo.com

"Make A Positive Impact On Your Life!"

"Jeanie Frankavitz shares her issues that she has had with negative or unethical people and how to overcome these challenges. The choices that we make effect the world and everyone around us, Frankavitz reminds us to stick to our morals, to be kind and respectful towards others. I would recommend this book to anyone looking to get rid of any despairing, gloomy feelings you may be having, looking to make a positive impact on your life and the people around you." --Katie Van Eynde, Author of *Motivate Your Magnetic Mind; 10 Simple Ways to Attract Positive Vibes In All Areas of Your Life,* KatieLovesLife.com

"One Book That You Must Have On Your Shelf!"

"*Don't Ask if You Don't Want to Know* by Jeanie Frankavitz is an inspiring cliff note of life's lessons. This is one book that you must have on your shelf." --Deb Woods

"Basic Truths In Successful Life Management!"

"Jeanie Frankavitz's personal reflections and home-style wisdoms illustrate some basic truths in successful life management. I felt like one of the family taking notes." --Linda LaBarba

"This Book Provides The Light!"

"Jeanie Frankavitz's words are cut-throat truths that we don't want to hear or very easily don't want to deal with. We hide behind the shadows of not wanting to face the reality but this book provides the light to it. *Don't Ask If You Don't Want to Know* is awesome, and definitely put a SMILE!" --Maggie Vargas

"Like Sitting Down With An Old Friend!"

"Enjoy Jeanie Frankavitz's new book ~ it's like sitting down with an old friend ~ kind, informative and trusting. *Don't Ask if You Don't Want to Know* is a thoughtful work that helps everyday folks make simple sense of our modern world. I strongly suggest you get a copy for yourself and for each of your circle of friends." --Patsy Perkins Quimby

CONTENTS

ACKNOWLEDGEMENTS

A.W. & Faye Oliver – The Grandparents every child should have; I was so lucky they were mine. My role models as a Grandparent and living my life the "right" way. I will be eternally grateful for knowing them and I am exceedingly honored to have them love me as much as they did and still do. They are always with me.

My dear Sister Judy – She continues to show me the meaning of sacrifice and love with her care for our Mother. She was my first friend and truly knows me better than I know myself.

Mom – Her life was different than it should have been, but she turned all the bad into magic. She continues to teach me every day how to live through adversity and never give up.

Shirley – Although she left us much too soon, her love lives on with those who remember. Friend, Mother-in-Law, and one of God's great gifts to the world. I treasure her memory and honor her life.

Lena – Always there to keep me on track when I faltered. Without you, this new chapter in my life would not have been possible.

Michael David and Gregory – Two of the three most important men in my life. My life is blessed beyond measure having sons such as you.

David – The most wonderful man I have ever known. Every day has been better than the last, all filled with joy and laughter. Thank you for finding me and turning my life into sunshine.

INTRODUCTION

Do you want to know how to be the best you can be? Do you want to know how to raise great children? Do you want to know how to have a great work life? Do you want to have a great marriage? Well, *Don't Ask If You Don't Want To Know*!

I am just an ordinary older woman, living an extraordinary life and amongst extraordinary people on this planet. I have learned so many things by trial and error, and have been honored to have made the mistakes that I hope you never have to make.

After many, many years of people, some even complete strangers, coming up to me asking why it is I smile all the time, close friends asking what the secret is to my marriage being so stable, and many asking why it is that they do not succeed in life, there was an obvious conclusion to make. Start telling them! I am going to share with you the wealth of life I have learned and pay it forward.

In the years I have lived, I have made more mistakes than I can count. That in mind, in most of those mistakes, I've truly absorbed the lesson that begged to be understood. I believe I have met the same obstacles most people have, but what sets my experiences apart, was my ability to not let them get to me. I have tried to rise above them, acknowledge their power, and use them to become a better human for this Earth.

I would hope you will use this as a guide to practical living. It is not rocket science, it is common sense reasoning that we all have, even though we don't all use it. Don't expect miracles; be a miracle. Don't wait for success; be successful.

HOW TO BE HAPPY

Happiness is that elusive objective for some, and a lifestyle for others. I've found it much easier to be happy in my life, than to dwell on those thoughts that bring me to sadness. Everyone has those bad days, or moments in their lives, but it's your decision how you choose to deal with those days and moments. I always told my children, that they can feel bad for themselves and pout and be upset and have a pity party for an hour, that is okay, but after that hour passes, they should look around them and evaluate the situation. Someone is always worse off than you are or is having a harder time with their lives than you are. That is not to say your sadness is invalid, but what that does imply is that you can and you will get over it.

To be sad is an overwhelming and frustrating emotion. Sadness can lead you to depression, physical illness, fatigue, and in some extreme forms, suicide. It's a vicious cycle that some people just cannot break and often times find themselves drowning in. We need to look towards ourselves and our children to break this cycle. Acts as simple as sharing a kind word, showing your smile, and reaching for a hug can bring someone back from the depths of sadness and turn their lives around.

One of the best pieces of advice I was ever given was, "Life isn't Fair." When my sons would complain that a rule or punishment wasn't "fair," I often told them they were right, because guess what? life isn't fair either and you better get used to it. I didn't do that to be mean or cruel, in fact, it would be cruel to keep them sheltered from the truth. I did it to prepare them for what would lie ahead when they become adults. Tears of sadness that life isn't fair can easily be molded into fierce determination to pave one's own way.

First and foremost, take that look around you. I can guarantee there are people near and dear to you with problems just as serious or much worse than your own. Give yourself ten minutes to totally immerse yourself in your problems and feel sorry for yourself. Set a timer if necessary. When that timer goes off, stop and think of three things you have in your life to be happy about. If it's your children, imagine their smiles and hugs. If it's your pet, time to snuggle. If it's your spouse, time for smiles, hugs, and snuggles (a triple treat). Then look around for a nursing home to visit. I guarantee that the smiles on those dear faces just having someone visiting them will make you forget about any problems you may be fixated on. Try volunteering at a food kitchen. The homeless population is growing much too fast and help is needed for serving food. Just let them know that someone cares. Share the smiles, spread the happiness anywhere and in any way possible.

To say I was raised in a dysfunctional family is an understatement. My childhood and family life could be an entirely other book on its own and I'm not alone in this. Many people my age were raised this way, but I refused to perpetuate the cycle. I used to be a single mother of two, so there were many times that I was depressed. If I was not depressed, I was hurt or scared. When I was in those moods, I had two wonderful boys that kept me busy. There is nothing like a little one asking their mommy to read them a story. That still melts my heart. I would drop anything to read to my boys. I may not have had the cleanest house, but my boys were most definitely well read. Spending time with them, no matter how long, lifted my spirit and let me know how wonderful it was to have them in my life. That is still the effect they have on me to this day.

Being happy is my state of Grace. The key to life is finding what makes you happy. The joy in letting someone know they must find their happiness is boundless. A co-worker of mine, many years ago, was just a miserable person. She was very nice, but very miserable. She had told me that one time she was looking for the perfect man to make her happy. I was stunned by what she had said and asked her what she had meant. She went into detail about how unhappy her life was. She was divorced, her kids were rotten, she didn't like her job, she couldn't find the right kind of men to date, the list went on. Then she made her big mistake, she asked me why I was happy and she wasn't? In the true spirit of *Don't Ask If You Don't Want To Know* I told her. The secret is very simple, learn to make yourself happy. No one is going to be able to do that for you. No matter how hard they try to make you happy, you won't reach happiness unless you get yourself there. The perfect man, perfect children, perfect job, are all just things, accessories to happiness. Nothing will make you happy if you don't know how to love yourself. She was stunned to say the least, but took it well. She eventually did seek professional help and after just a few months, everyone noticed a positive change in her attitude. I haven't seen her in a while, but I have heard she is remarried and truly happy!

You can be a lost soul or you can be the saver of lost souls; your choice. It's much more rewarding to give than to receive, and that's a fact, not just a trite old saying. When you are feeling sorry for yourself and find yourself being unhappy, don't blame others. Stand up and look in the mirror and see that *you* are ultimately responsible for *you*! Get off your backside and do something for someone, anyone, as long as you're doing something. Try to volunteer at a pet shelter. I guarantee it will put a smile on your face. Be a helper at school, your children will love you for it.

Give the gift of yourself this year. You will be a much better person for it.

JOURNAL YOUR THOUGHTS

What can you do to make a difference in your life and be happy? List 5 things that will make you happy. No, a new Mercedes won't do it; take this seriously! Be giving of yourself to achieve true happiness.

HOW TO GAIN
RESPECT AND KEEP IT

It's an old adage that "you earn respect, it isn't given." That is a very true statement. If you treat others the way you want to be treated, with respect and with dignity, chances are you'll get that very same respect back. Honesty and fairness in personal or business relationships are key. In my many years on this good Earth, I have found that people mainly behave the same in both their personal and their business lives. If you are an untrustworthy cheat and a liar in business, the odds are high that your personal relationships are treated in a similar fashion.

Too many people today do not seem to care whether or not they are respected. My husband has always said to our children and Grandchildren "you have two things that are yours: your name and your word. Don't lose either of them." By that he means people remember you and what you say. It is very easy to lose respect, and extremely difficult to get it back.

You are judged by your actions and your words. If you spend your life not being honest with yourself, how can you be honest with others? Lots of young people shoplift or take things that don't belong to them. Most parents and adults look at this as a rite of passage or just a childish act that comes with a so-called rebellious stage. That is wrong! What that is theft, point blank. This mindset sets children up for a lifetime of conflict and dishonesty. Children must be taught from a very early age that you do not take anything that doesn't belong to you. Period. Lying is another whitewash we've been allowing in our society. There is no such thing as a little white lie. Masking it to downplay its consequences has such a negative effect on our children, and the adults they grow up to be. A lie is a lie. End of story.

If you do not respect yourself, you cannot expect others to respect you. You would be surprised how many people have little to no self-respect. If you are a single parent, it is vital that you respect yourself in your daily life. Young children are like sponges and are extremely susceptible to soak up anything and everything they witness. They will notice if Mommy or Daddy are not acting respectfully to each other, and almost always the behavior that the parents exhibit will be mimicked by their kids. We are the teachers and we must set a good example to all around us.

I have learned that respect is the key to success. Everyone comes to a "fork in the road" and I learned early on that the road less traveled may be longer and certainly more interesting, but it is not necessarily the road to being a respectable person.

An employer was "interested" in one of the younger females in the office. After months of his unwanted advances and requests to please leave her alone, she had enough and went home early. The next morning she arrived at the office with her dad and older brother, both of whom were very built and strong. He asked to see the employer, both went into the office, closed the door and had a discussion. After a few minutes the door opened, her dad and older brother doffed their hats to the other ladies in the room and left the office. The girl's employer rang and went in to his "how dare you let them in, they could have killed me, I have a reputation, etc." She said, you HAD a reputation, that's why they came in. Her dad was not going to put up with his daughter being treated in this manner. He expected her to be shown respect in the work place and saw to it that she did. There was never another incident and this young lady became more confident simply due to the respect she was given and the self-respect she had for herself!

Respect in relationships is crucial. Your relationship may not be working out and the opportunity to stray is creeping into your mind. This is never okay. If you are at the point in the relationship that you feel like stepping over the line, remember to have enough respect for your partner to end it beforehand. It may be difficult to say: "you know, this isn't working out and before something happens that shouldn't, I feel I will need to leave," but it is necessary. By doing so, you have shown your partner (who by the way won't understand this at all at the time, but will one day) that the relationship is over, but the respect for you as a person stands. It also gives you the self-respect you will need to go forward.

Self-respect is important in every aspect of life, be it personal or business. Your confidence will no doubt receive a boost, as well you understanding that you possess the respect of others.

Respect is the cornerstone of your personality, don't chip it.

JOURNAL YOUR THOUGHTS

List 5 ways you can respect others and yourself.

_____

_____

_____

_____

_____

_____

_____

_____

_____

_____

HOW TO BE A GOOD
CITIZEN OF THE WORLD

Hate and mistrust have always been problems in this world. I was raised by parents who had two different ideas of racism. My mother was an open-minded woman who never allowed my sister, brother or me to be unkind or uncaring to anyone. My father on the other hand wasn't quite on the same page. We're all put here on this planet for a reason. Our job is to discover that reason. Helping our fellow citizens reach their full potential only helps us in return.

This world is ever-changing and growing more dangerous each day. The only way to make a change in our world is by first making a change in ourselves. There is so much simplicity in just treating others the way we want to be treated. If everyone did just that, imagine how quickly the horrors in this world stop? My guess: overnight.

My Grandfather's family moved from Tennessee to Oklahoma, then known as Indian Territory, in 1900. They traveled all those miles in a covered wagon seeking a better life. Did they find it? They became sharecropper's on a farm owned by African Americans who also came to Oklahoma for a better life. Did they find it? Two families from the South trying to raise their children in less than ideal conditions. I believe their story is the story of the world. My Grandfather became a school teacher, a Judge of the local county, a business owner, and a minister. He respected all religions, races, and economic statuses. When we are all respectful of others, we can really become good citizens.

Helping each other through times of trouble is exceedingly important. No matter how small the effort, helpful acts makes a difference. How many times have you walked down the street or noticed someone in your office that looks sad and depressed? It is so simple just to offer a smile. That simple act can change someone's world. I would like to think it could really change the entire world.

Helping someone through dark times can be the light that very well might save their life. We've discussed being a saver of souls earlier, and it can also be to our own well-being. The world is so full of self-serving people who have no time for those who are in need or anyone who needs a hand-up in life. I have spent my life's journey trying to help anyone I could and I will never stop doing so. The gratification I get is greater than any gift I could possibly imagine. By helping, I don't mean doing the job for them or living their lives for them. It is as simple as being there for the person, whether it be spiritual, physical, or emotional support, support is essential.

I remember as a child it seemed like everyone had a pen-pal. The idea of bringing the world together through letters was something that excited me! After World War II, with everything in such chaos, young people had little hope for the future. Schools here and abroad joined together in bridging those fears by simply writing back and forth to each other. I even knew some people who kept up these letter relationships and met each other as adults, bringing their lives closer and making us realize we really aren't that different from each other.

Everyone wants to live in a place where they can feel safe and happy and we must learn that since world leaders cannot do this for us, we must do it for ourselves. I have always tried to learn as much as I could about different cultures and religions. My Grandfather was a minister, and one of his requests was that we should all visit other holy places of worship and learn as much as we could about all of their religions. I remember as a child going to a Baptist revival with a friend of mine. When the altar call was made, I was Johnny-on-the-spot to the front of the church to be saved, three times in one week. I recall the Baptist pastor calling my dear Grandfather, a Methodist minister, and saying how much he appreciated my attendance, but was fairly certain I was already saved. He asked why I felt the need to do this and I had to tell the truth. The truth was that my friend would get a Ten Commandment bracelet if she had the most "saves". I really wanted her to have it.

This is the only world we have and it must be saved. I grew up living during the Cold War and really do not want to have the "bunker" mentality take over my Grandchildren's lives.

Help each other heal the world.

JOURNAL YOUR THOUGHTS

List 5 examples of how you can make a difference in the world.

HOW TO BE A

VALUABLE EMPLOYEE

Help your boss succeed. If your boss is a jerk, help him or her become a better person by acting as an example. Always do the right thing and never compromise your ethics or morals for anyone. If you are asked to do something that you know is wrong, take a moment to ask yourself if you really need to hurt yourself in this way. The answer should be no. You can always find another work position, but if you lose yourself, you lose everything.

We are not perfect. We all want more, think that we know best, and assume that we could do better than those around us. There are people we work with daily that we do not really care for or like. Personality conflicts are human nature, but it is how we handle these conflicts that define us. We do not have to like the people we work with, but we owe them the respect of being a fellow employee and should be able to put up with them.

The business world is a difficult place now. Nothing is guaranteed, and it is no longer a badge of honor to be at the same company for thirty years. In the business climate of today, you are only as secure as you make yourself. At any given moment, you can be moved to another manager, across town, or even across the country. You must not only do your job effectively, but proactively. Be prepared is not just the Boy Scout motto, it very much resonates in business as well.

Always be the person that can be counted on to do the right thing. Nothing is worse than having a fellow employee fail to pull their weight while you get stuck with all the work and they get the glory. Eventually, the employee not pulling their weight will lose their footing. It might take a while, but it will always catch up with them. It's called Karma. It can be ugly when it happens, you may not be there to see it, but it will happen in some way or another. For years I struggled with stress in trying to be the best employee no matter what. I was fortunate that I lived through it! I also learned that the best employee is not necessarily the one that is out front. It is the person that can be counted on to get the job done in a timely manner no matter what, and without compromise.

Having simple rules to follow will make a huge difference when it comes to business. Rules apply to everyone and everyone should be required to follow them. Your job is to know the rules, and follow them.

For years I have struggled with stress in trying to be the best employee no matter what. I was fortunate that I lived through it! I also learned that the best employee is not necessarily the one that is out front, but rather the one that can be counted on to get the job done in a timely manner, without compromise.

Do you want to be the person who changes a financial to make things look better for the boss? Do not compromise your morals or ethics to make someone like you better because they won't. You become the go to person for "changes," but don't think for a minute they are thinking about what a great person you are. You are just the unethical person helping them along in their unethical way of doing business. Trust me, you'll be out of there as soon as possible.

Always be the person that can be counted on to do the right thing. Your self-confidence will soar and your happiness within will shine.

Do not compromise your morals and ethics, that's all you have.

JOURNAL YOUR THOUGHTS

What can you do to be a better employee? List 5 things you could do today at work that will have a positive impact on your company and your well-being.

HOW TO BE A
VALUABLE EMPLOYER

Be fair, honest, direct, and do not show favoritism. Favoritism breeds jealousy among your team which will ultimately bring you down. It's the bad sports team analogy. If a team doesn't like their coach, they will play badly until eventually the coach gets replaced. Don't be that bad coach.

Your employees can make or break your company. You do not need to cater to their every whim, but you do need treat them with respect and common courtesy. Do not berate or humiliate your employee because it does reflect directly back to you. Yelling at your team immediately turns them off to you and their work. Your message will most likely be lost and ignored if spoken through anger and shouts. Your employees will completely miss the point of your yelling and you will lose your voice both figuratively and physically.

Your employees will make or break you and your company. There was a management style in the 80's known by many as "management by intimidation." This style called for literally terrifying the employee into doing their job your way, or else. The outcome: not very effective. There is no book to tell you the correct way to guide employees other than the good old fashioned "Golden Rule." Treat others the way you want to be treated. There is no other way to truly get results and be successful.

Implement an environment of harmony at your place of business. Your employees are the lifeblood of your success and it is in your best interest to ensure everything runs as smooth as possible. Make sure your employees know you care about them, about their work, and about their future. Their future, essentially, is your future.

As discussed in the previous chapter, the same goes for the employer as the employee. We have all had those employers that asked us to do things we didn't feel were right. Don't be that person! Never ask someone to do something that you wouldn't do yourself. As a leader, you have certain responsibilities to your staff, honesty being the most important. Asking your team to compromise themselves in any way also touches on the chapter on Respect.

The employer making advances towards the young lady in our office was a perfect example. He asked many times for us to lie to his wife while he was off doing something he should not have been doing, with someone he should not have been doing it with. Some of the staff was willing to do so, I was not. My response always was, then you better hope I don't answer the phone if she calls. I will not now, nor ever cover up for bad behavior. It doesn't make anything better, in fact it will certainly make it worse. Working in that environment was stressful and not conducive to good mental health for anyone concerned. I left there with a happy heart and never looked back. Respect your employees, they are the backbone of your company.

JOURNAL YOUR THOUGHTS

What can you do for your Company and its employees? List 5 things as a business owner you can improve to make your company a winner.

_____

_____

_____

_____

_____

_____

_____

_____

_____

_____

_____

_____

HOW TO HAVE A
HAPPY MARRIAGE

Like your spouse. I know you love them, but liking them is just as important. I am married to my best friend. We love to be together, but we are also individuals who can function apart from each other. We are together because we want to be, not because we have to be. We value our friendship as much as our love for each other.

Treat your spouse like your best friend and your marriage will last forever! A strong statement, but one I have found to be true. Think about it, you tell your best friend your deepest secrets, so why wouldn't you share the same with your spouse? You would never cheat on your best friend, so why would you cheat on your spouse? You would never lie to your best friend, so why would you lie to your spouse?

This is the person you are spending your entire life with. This person needs to be someone who is going to share your happiness, your failures, your hopes, and your dreams with. You will not always pick the right person. This is not to say that marriage is similar to a business relationship, but do your due diligence. It is necessary to put emotions aside and ask yourself if this person will help you attain your goals in life. Also, do you want to help this person attain their goals in life? Each are mutually important. Marriage is a two way street, and both partners need to be on the same side of the road when traveling or there will be an inevitable crash.

One thing I know for sure is marriage is an ongoing project. There are endless pitfalls and challenges that sometime may appear too difficult to maintain a loving and caring relationship. Every couple has their ups and downs and that can be difficult, but nothing is more rewarding than a happy relationship. I was given some advice many years ago that really does work. You cannot yell and scream if you're holding your partners hand. Sounds very simple, doesn't it? Well, I can tell you, it works.

I wish I could tell you the secret to my marriage, but I do not really know what it is. All I know is that my husband and I have a relationship based on mutual respect, deep love, and most importantly, we are best friends. Having gone through a failed marriage and my fair share of bad relationships in the past, I couldn't have been more thrilled, happy and safe with my perfect man who walked into my life offering friendship and respect. He knew instinctively I needed a friend first, now thirty years later, he is still my best friend, husband of the year, and the person who taught me what true love really is.

Someone asked me once how I knew he was the one. It's something you can't describe other than "that's the way it should make you feel." That is the only way I can put it, it's the way love should make you feel. I have been given a lot of advice in my life about finding the right one. An older relative told me I should ask myself if I was willing to spend the rest of my life cleaning the toilet after him. And you know what, I am! When you're ready, you're ready.

Love is one of those emotions that will hurt you if you aren't careful. Watch your heart because it's very fragile. Trust your instincts as much as you can, but (here's that word again) never compromise your ethics. To young ladies thinking about making the decision to have sex because "he said if I loved him I would do that for him," I would ask yourself, what is it you want? Is that what *you* want to do? Most would answer no, but just feel the pressure to go all the way, as we used to say. If a girl isn't sure or doesn't want to, then she needs to be told "if he loved you, he wouldn't want you to do anything you don't want to do." Emotions and hormones always play a large role and teenage years are a very difficult time of life to be sure.

Be sure you protect your heart, no one else can do that for you.

JOURNAL YOUR THOUGHTS

What can you do to improve your marriage today? List 5 things you can do to make your spouse smile today. It always starts with a smile.

HOW TO RAISE
RESPONSIBLE CHILDREN

They are so cute when they are little. Then they become teenagers and you wonder who these people are and what have they done with the cute little babies you once knew. Do not try to be your child's best friend, they have plenty of people to fill those roles, but not many to fill your parental role. Don't wait until they are teenagers to instill discipline and manners. Children need to know their boundaries and limits, and ultimately must be told and assured they are loved daily.

You have one chance to raise your children. Unfortunately, they don't come with handbooks, and not each model is created identically, so for the most part, each of us are on our own. There is however, a fairly simple rule if you think about it. Treat your kids the way you wanted to be treated as a child. Did you really want to be given everything? Did you really want to go everywhere? Did you really want no rules? Answer honestly and you'll find that most rules are given from care and love. Parents don't come down on kids because they hate them, they do it out of love.

There are too many incidents of the younger generation committing horrible acts upon each other and themselves. It is trite to say ask where their parents are? Didn't they see the signs? What happened at home? After raising two boys that turned into wonderful men (I can tell you it is not an easy task), the one thing I know is this: love and discipline is key. You cannot allow them to make their own rules and run their own show. My parents both worked and I can tell you, no one got away with anything even when they were not at home. We had set things that needed to be done by the time they got home and we did them no questions asked. No whining, no tears, no arguments. Rules were set and rules were followed and that's how it's supposed to be.

Violence in children, in my opinion, is a direct result of what they see and hear. So many kids today are "raised" by video games. At a very early age they are being desensitized by the violence surrounding them in games, film, and music. Let me just put this out there, ratings were created for a reason! There is a major component of parental neglect involved, when parents do not supervise what their children are watching or doing. If you choose to allow these games to be played by your children, then by all means, sit and watch them while they play. Chances are you will put a halt in their gaming, or at least slow-down what they are doing and reevaluate.

At one point in my youngest sons life (mid 1980's), he wanted a pair of Air Jordan shoes. He wanted those shoes so badly, but they were about $100 a pair. His argument was that everybody had a pair and he had to be like everybody else. It seemed like a totally understandable want for a 15-year-old child, but things for us were very tight and we really didn't see the need to spend that excessive amount of money on a pair of shoes that he'll most likely grow out of. We sat him down and listened to the reasons he "needed" those shoes. Then my husband made what I thought was a life altering decision. He explained that we normally would spend $50 on a pair of shoes so he would be perfectly willing to give our son the reasonable $50 for the shoes, and if our son was willing to put in the other $50 from his own money, he'd be able to get the shoes. Well, now that's a shoe on the other foot, pardon the pun. Suddenly he was forced to think about it. He wasn't so sure he really "needed" the pair of shoes after all. The need wasn't as obvious since it wasn't something easily accessible, he learned it wasn't necessary to get. He didn't buy the shoes, but instead learned a very valuable lesson. He really had to decide how bad he wanted something and ultimately learned the difference between "needing" and "wanting".

The difference of needing and wanting has now been passed on to my Grandchildren. A very valuable lesson for every child to learn. I wonder how many troubled children have not made the distinction in needing and wanting something. As parents, we always want to give our children everything, but that isn't always the right thing to do. What does that teach our children? In my opinion, it leads them to believe they are entitled to whatever they want, however they can get it. Parents are inclined to protect their children as they should, but not at the expense of society. Witness the lengths parents go to in order to provide whatever Little Johnny or Jane wants. They will steal, lie, cheat, beat fellow shoppers on Black Friday (which is why I never leave the house on that day) just so they are viewed as heroes. The act of providing the latest horrifying video game for their precious child will continue the cycle of children who have no idea what the value of a dollar is, and will just whine and cry if they don't get what they want.

My theory is that when children were given the upper hand of no punishment in schools or at home, they were unintentionally taught that they were in charge. When parents decide to be best friends with their kids, they are unconsciously failing to guide them into adulthood. Children are raising themselves because parents are not utilizing the skills they have in order to correct the bad behavior. I would never and have never been a proponent of corporal punishment, but I will say I think a child has a lot of extra fat on their behinds for a reason. From age two to around age eight, a swift smack on the hiney could be necessary to let them know what their limits are.

Be a parent, your kids have enough friends. Which also leads me to the next chapter!

JOURNAL YOUR THOUGHTS

How can you make your child a more responsible person? List 5 things you can do to help your child accept responsibility.

HOW TO DISCIPLINE
YOUR CHILDREN

I was raised during a time when corporal punishment was the belt, a switch, or a slap by anyone in your family whether it be your parents, grandparents, aunts, uncles, etc. If a neighbor saw that a child was doing something wrong, the child would get it from the neighbor first, and then their parents when they got home. They got away with nothing. I survived that form of punishment and, perhaps, it even made me a better person. That being said, I raised my children differently, with other methods of punishment, and those methods worked just as well. The important thing was that my children always knew I meant business. They respected my authority and knew what they could and could not do. Consistency with authority is key!

Discipline is effective as long as it's combined with love, rather than with anger. There are very effective ways to discipline that do not involve physical contact. Time-out can be effective for some children, while lectures can be effective for others. You must find the most effective punishment in order for your child to understand the point you are trying to make. If your child writes on a wall, make him clean it off. Trust me, your kid will think twice next time if they have the memory of an hour spent with a pail and sponge scrubbing a wall in the back of their house. The purpose isn't to be cruel, it is to teach the child that what they did was wrong, so that action is never repeated.

Too many children today are running wild with absolutely no guidance, and it shows. From a very early age they are allowed to run rampant in stores, restaurants, movie theaters, and certainly in the home. Kids who lack boundaries will not learn how to behave when they become adults. What you see at age four is going to be very similar to what you will see when they are twenty, only ten times worse. Parents think it is cute to hear curse words and see their kids throwing temper tantrums when they are young. Some even go so far as giddily posting their kids inappropriate behavior on social media for the world to see, thinking of it as a form of entertainment. Then, before they know it, they find themselves sitting in a courtroom or visiting that child in prison twenty years later wondering what happened. Poor parenting has decimated this society. It is not the lack of funds that ruins children, it is the lack of guidance and parenting skills.

Children are our future, period. There are no ifs, ands, or buts about it. People are constantly talking about how bad kids are. Questions are thrown out like: what's wrong with kids today, how did this happen to my kid, why does each generation get worse and worse, etc. We must deal with these problems when they are young before they are old enough to completely ruin their lives or the lives of those around them.

Children today are being taught by parents, schools, and the government, that they are in complete control of their own bodies and are entitled to protection. They are taught that they should report anyone they are afraid of or anyone who is hurting them. That is a very important thing for all children to know; they can ask for help from anyone in order to feel safe. Our kids safety and well being is always priority. That in mind, one might wonder by doing so, have we given away our rights as parents to discipline our children? When you raise your voice to your teenager and use a corrective tone can he tell his school counselor he is being abused at home? When you ground your child for unruly behavior or breaking the rules, can he report this to the school or authorities? If you swat your misbehaving youngster on the backside to get his attention, can he inform the school he is being beaten? The answer to all of these questions is yes. Parents are increasingly being put in the position of trying to correct a teenager and being told, "you can't tell me what to do" or "you can't yell at me, I'll call Child Protective Services". This happens every day. Recently in the news, an eighteen year old girl moved out of her parents home because she did not like the rules. She then sued them to try and get school expenses and tuition. Luckily, the judge was sound minded and agreed with the parents and gave the young girl and her attorneys a stern lecture about her unrealistic wants and inappropriate behavior. Although the law doesn't intend to set up scenarios like this, it does happen and it happens often.

You must take the time to find the proper punishment that works. With my boys, I knew early on I had no intention of breaking blood vessels on my hand against a pair of jean rivets. Trial and error will allow you to come up with what works for you and your child. I am not a fan of corporal punishment, but there are some children that need a good swat every now and then on their behinds. I'm not talking about raising them off the floor or leaving a mark, but just enough to get their attention. This is usually effective up to about the age of six. Then your work really sets in for you. Is it time-out? Is it sitting in a corner? Is it sending them to their room? I tried many methods on my boys. A good deterrent was a paddle ball paddle. If you remember them, the rubber band and ball will always come off quickly. I never used it, but would take it down occasionally and smack my leg with it. Makes an awful sound, but gets the attention and calms the situation. However, the punishment that brought my oldest to his knees was, now get ready for it, writing sentences! He has asked me many times if I would just spank him and get it over with instead of making him write SENTENCES!

My oldest son was very much like I was at his age. He always had to have the last word. If I said "no more talking", he would say "OK". If I said not another word, he'd reply with "Yes, Ma'am," just to spite me. When he was about twelve, he entered his "smart-mouth" stage and boy, could he pull some zingers. After one particular incident, I had enough and proceeded to tell him that he had to write sentences! I formulated a doozy something to the effect of: "I know I was disrespectful to my Mother, this is totally unacceptable behavior from me and I will endeavor to never act this way again."

Now, anyone who has ever had to write sentences, then you know this was not the type of sentence desired by the perpetrator. He had a little notebook just for sentences and spent many, many hours writing away. This actually led him to have to think about each word he wrote and it evidently made an impression. When I was helping him unpack when he returned from the Army much later in life, I found one of the books in his bag. I asked him what he was doing with it? He looked at me and said it had such an impact on his life that he always had it with him so he would do the right thing. I tell you, Parents, when they are children the most wonderful three words are "I Love You." When they are adults those most wonderful words are joined by three others: "You Were Right." I have been fortunate to hear those words from both of my children.   I am a Happy Mommy.

I had a very good friend in New Jersey who complained continually about how she could not get her pre-teen son to do anything without throwing a fit. She yelled constantly and all she got for her trouble was a sore throat of course and continued bad behavior. She did the smacking around, also to no avail. I mentioned the sentences to her and told her she had nothing to lose.   I explained to her that in my opinion kids totally turn of yelling knowing you'll be quiet eventually. She said she would give it a try and low and behold 3 weeks later she had a "new child". He hated the punishment so would do whatever not to have to write all those sentences.   Even if it meant he had to behave! Success at last!

You will instantly decompress. No tears, no screaming, no banging of doors (how many times did you open and close a screen door as a child before you got the idea?), just quiet literary genius at the kitchen table. As I stated previously, children learn from their parents from a very early age how to behave. Look at your own behavior reflected in your child. Are you a screamer? Chances are your child is as well. Do you throw things around? Chances are your child has an arm on him the Major Leagues would be happy to sign. Sentences are a method to help you both. You become a calmer parent, the child becomes calmer and more obedient. Double win.

Discipline is necessary and must be tempered with love.

JOURNAL YOUR THOUGHTS

List 5 ways you can discipline your child (without being thrown in jail or appear on an abuse registry).

HOW TO BE A
GOOD FRIEND

Friendship is a lot like marriage, you have to nurture and care for it like any strong relationship requires. Be honest with your friends, never lie to them, never intentionally hurt them, and always be there for them.

True friends are not easy to find. They must be those people who will compliment your life rather than bringing ill feelings, or sadness upon it. They must be able to lift you up to be the best you can be. They must be there for you in the bad times, as well as the good. Never forget this goes both ways, you cannot have good friends unless you are a good friend yourself.

With the world in such turmoil, we need to have someone we can share life's joys and sorrows. If you are married to your best friend, well then that's great! If you are single, you really should have a support group to help you through life's challenges. We need our friends as mentors, guides, and helpers, to navigate through the rough spots and to celebrate with us at the top of the mountain.

Be there for your friends. If you notice a problem, don't pry, but ask if there is anything you can do for them. Just listening can make such a difference in their lives and yours. I am not a "buttinsky" (though some of my friends may differ on that), but they all know, *"Don't Ask If You Don't Want To Know!"*

I have been fortunate in my life to have worked in many industries from medical, construction, manufacturing, telecommunications, and so on, and I have enjoyed each and every job I have had and have made many, many friends from all over the world. These friends are so very dear to me and I have kept in touch with as many as possible. What I have learned is that friends are the same no matter where they are from. Their basic needs are just like yours, their families are just like yours, their problems are just like yours. The most important thing you can do is treat your friends like you want to be treated. That old Golden Rule is back for another go around. They don't need to be treated as children, or to be spoken to in a condescending fashion.

They just want to be with people like themselves with the same morals and ethics they also live by.

Try to be the best friend you can be. There are so many out there that need a friend. Even those who don't think they do, need a friend. You can change a life with your words, both for the better or the worse. As with any relationship trust is tantamount. If that trust is broken, then good luck mending those fences. Should you do something to damage your friendship and decide that you want to try and salvage it, then you must admit what you have done to cause the damage and apologize for it. Saying "I'm Sorry" is not as difficult as it sounds and will make you a much better person for doing so.

Chances are you will find a happiness and joy in friendship you did not know even existed.

Friends are much too important to lose for no reason. Work at keeping friends, they are worth it.

JOURNAL YOUR THOUGHTS

How can I be a better friend? List 5 things you can do for a friend to make them know you care.

_____

_____

_____

_____

_____

_____

_____

_____

_____

_____

_____

HOW TO BE THE BEST PERSON YOU CAN BE

Take care of yourself first. That sounds selfish, but if you don't then how can you be there for those who love you? You are so important to this world and have so much to give to others; it is your duty to be the best person you can be, if not for you, then for them. Be honest with yourself. Never hurt anyone. And most importantly: smile. Even if you feel lousy, smile. You will be surprised how easy that one act is, and how much better it will make you feel. Those around you will return that smile with smiles in return. See how far the smiles spread, and where that can take us collectively as a whole.

It is not easy to be a good person. If we had more good people in this world, it would be a much better place. There are so many chances to do the wrong thing in life instead of the good, and often times, the bad may seem like the easier option. We must take action to avoid the wrong and stand up for ourselves to be better. Helping those around us not only helps the less fortunate, but helps us to be better, as well.

The world needs more "good" people in it, because we have plenty of bad ones out there. It is easy to sit around and wait for someone else to take the lead on doing the right thing. The horrors of this world are endless, joys become more rare, and despair overtakes us. Multiply this by the billions of people on this Earth, and we quickly become a world no one wants to be a part of, with nowhere to go to escape it. We are quickly going down that path and the time has come to reverse it. Sound simple? Not quite, but it can be done.

Set a good example for others. You may say that is too simple. I tell you that it is not. Being the best you can be is how to change the world. It takes a lot of work to think of horrible things to do to people, not so much to be kind. Again, it is the Golden Rule at work. Do Unto Others As You Would Have Them Do Unto You. Not only is this a simple way to live, this mentality can change the world.

Being a good person is not something you wake up one morning and decide. There is no light switch to flip, it takes a lot of thought. You know what they say: It takes more muscles to frown than it does to smile. It also takes more time to think of the negative thing to say or do than to just smile and go about the business of being nice.

We have all worked with that person at work who is just not "right." No matter what you do, no matter what anyone does, nothing is going to make the situation any easier. I will tell you this. Rise to the occasion and take the opportunity to help that person. No one knows what is going on in someone else's mind or thoughts. I'm not saying to be allow yourself to be a victim, but be a diffuser if possible. When things are going bad for no reason, a verbal (or physical for that matter) hug can sometimes make the difference. A simple email to that person offering "it seems you're not having a good day, let me know if I can help with anything" can literally diffuse a very bad situation in the making. You could take them a cup of tea or coffee with a smile. A smile is the first thing a new baby sees and I believe it is imprinted in our minds as a trigger to soothe and calm us. A subliminal sedative, if you will.

Having worked in the private sector for over forty years, I've run into some strange situations and some even stranger people. I worked with one individual who continually had a nasty, nasty attitude and just continued to bait people daily to get, in my opinion his daily charge of adrenalin. One of my coworkers had to meet with him on a particular rough day and she was dreading it. I had been through it and just told her if he started trying to her to argue with him, just look him square in the eye, get up and say: "I can see you're not feeling well. We can continue our meeting when you feel better." Then leave the office and go back to her desk. She took total control of the situation, stood her ground, and took my suggestion. She never had the problem again, he showed the utmost respect for her, as he did me, and moved on to other employees. I have no idea how long it took him to realize we were telling everyone to repeat the same thing when he started getting angry. It was very empowering for all of us and he eventually left the company.

Be aware of your fellow co-workers. You may be spending up to ten hours a day, five days a week with these people, so you should better be learning how to get along with them. They can become your worst enemies or your best friends; that depends on the dynamics of the environment and how you chose to interact. I choose to try my best to befriend those I'm with daily, but it can be difficult at times as any relationship can. The key is respect; your respect for others, and their respect for you.

Whatever you can do in life to help another, you are benefitting two – them and you. SMILE!

JOURNAL YOUR THOUGHTS

How can I be a better person today? List 5 ways you can improve yourself and be the person you want to be.

NOW THAT YOU KNOW

I want to thank you for reading this little book of "me-isms." That is really all it is, the musings and reactions I have experienced now that I have reached my Golden Years of life. None of us are born with a handbook, so we are raised by people who really have no clue what they are doing and if they were working in the private sector would be fired immediately for some of their results. My parents did the best they could based on what they knew. Times were different then, of course, but they did what they could. We did the same thing with our children; the best we could. Some don't meet that challenge of doing their best to raise their children, and the rest of us suffer the consequences.

We are all here on this Earth for a very short time and most of us never realize what our purpose is or think how our lives affect those around us. In my opinion, and you know by now, *Don't Ask*

If You Don't Want To Know. We all interact with each other from the moment we open our eyes in some way or another. Ever wonder what if? What if you had not stopped to check if the coffeepot was turned off? Would that 15 seconds have meant it would have been you in the accident at the intersection you drive through every morning? How many lives were affected by your stopping to check the coffeepot? Think about it. Not many people do think about it and that is why, again my opinion, so many thoughtless actions occur. Just stop and think before you act or say something that might affect someone else. It really can be just that easy. The greatest joy in life is realizing your purpose. It could be as simple as you were supposed to check your coffeepot and not be in the accident because that person may have needed to be seen by a physician. They wouldn't go on their own, now they have to be taken to the hospital and a lifesaving procedure performed. Far-fetched? Maybe. But, what if that is the way life is? Far-fetched.

The importance of your life and how it affects those around you is not to be taken lightly. Ever. Being kind to others, respectful to those with whom you work, helpful to those around you, raising productive children, being a good citizen of the world is the basis of ensuring your happiness in life. Will there be struggles, pitfalls, hardships? Yes, of course, but the real meaning of life is in overcoming those battles and coming out smiling. Wearing the "Smile of Life" can do more to heal your ills than a lot of medication. Understanding your life and what you are to accomplish in it cannot be pushed aside or held back. It should be like a train coming down the tracks at 100 mph. People need to get out of the way or get run over by your life and how you plan to live it.

I have alluded to my childhood briefly. Perhaps one day I will put what I can on paper. I will say first that it was not easy. The older I get I realize how difficult it was. I was a child of the 50's raised by children of the late 30's and 40's. They in turn were raised by children of the War to end all Wars, WWI, and so on.

Everyone who knows me well, knows my love of history and, particularly, genealogy. Realizing the difficulties of those who came before helped me understand the whys and hows of my parents lives. I was blessed with Grandparents on my Mother's side who were the role models of my life. I don't mean to take away from my Father's side of the family, it is just fact. I realize now that my parents were children raising children. They had not had the opportunities to experience social interactions with a variety of people, live with different cultures, travel, basically how to deal with life. Their struggles became our struggles. They worked hard, did the best they could with what they had. My Grandparents had the same struggles, but managed differently. No matter what problem, no matter how difficult life became, no matter what was thrown at them.....they were happy. They simply looked for the good in people and the good in life.

Always happy and smiling, they spread their love and joy to all around them, at least to my way of looking at it. I realized later in life that joy can be found in anything you do.

By looking at life not as "what it can do for me", but "what can I do to make this better", you can turn any situation into a plus. Are you a bystander in life? Do you watch while others pave the way for you? Perhaps you should try to be the first one in the pool and set the example for others. If you choose to enter into a long term relationship with someone, don't let them be the leader. It takes two to have a relationship, friendship or marriage, and should take two to make it work. If you choose to have children, don't expect them to be born knowing how to behave, how to learn, how to be a good person that will make you proud. You should realize that little blob of cells will eventually be roaming this earth with the rest of us making decisions affecting all of us.

Parenting is the most important job on this Earth, again in my opinion. Next time you are at a restaurant after 8 p.m. and there are children under 5 running around tripping wait-staff and causing horrendous interruptions in your nice evening out, stop and think what goes on at home for them. I guarantee that child was not born that way. That child is a product of parents who don't care about others around them and are raising that child to also not care. You will see that child affect the world in many ways and probably not in a good way.

Being a happy, caring, sharing person not only helps yourself, but ultimately affects....me! If more people are happy, doing the right thing that means the rest of us who try to do it right can relax a little.

Ask yourself what you can do to add to the humanity of this world. Don't sit by and wait for someone else to act, get up and do something!! It really is a simple concept, so simple it is usually discounted. But, I will tell you this....try it and see if it doesn't make your life easier and happier:

Smile even if you don't feel like. You'll have less wrinkles and feel lighter.

Raise your children to be honest, respectful, caring individuals.

Be the best you can be in this world, no matter what it takes, and no matter how hard it is. You are here for a reason. Your job is to find out what that reason is and fulfill your destiny.

FREQUENTLY ASKED QUESTIONS

Is it possible to be truly happy?

Of course! Is it easy? Well, that depends on your attitude and what you truly consider as happiness. Happiness is a state of mind; what makes one person happy can be much less than what makes another happy.

Can one person really make a difference?

As I write this, Nelson Mandela has recently passed away. Think about his accomplishments as one person and ask yourself the question again. Obviously, yes! One person can make an enormous difference in this world, and that one person can be you!

Why should I care if people respect me or not?

You only have one opportunity to make a first impression. How many times have you heard that? Well, you hear it so often for a reason; it's true! If people don't respect you, things in your life become just plain difficult. You will be ignored, passed over for promotions, lose good friends, and basically not have much of a life. Respect is very under-rated as a trait and is actually one of the most valuable gifts you can give yourself and others.

How can I make my boss notice me at work?

Do your best every day. Sounds simple, doesn't it? Well, the purpose of a job is being paid to do your best, so naturally that is what one would do. Put yourself in your boss's position. Would you pay for a poor performance? Of course not. And neither will your boss for very long.

How can I help my employees do their best?

Do your best every day. Sounds like the same answer to question 4, right? It is the same concept. Help your employees bring their best by bringing yours. No one want to work, let alone wants to do their best working for an angry, nasty, person who's difficult to please. Put yourself in your employees position. You wouldn't put up with it either.

How can I make my relationship stronger?

Trust and respect. Treat your spouse/significant other with the same respect and care your do your friends. Think to yourself "would I treat a stranger this way" or "would I say that to a friend"? Don't take your relationship for granted.

How do I raise responsible children in this ever-changing world?

Being a good role model is key. If your children see or hear you lie, cheat, or steal, then don't be surprised when they imitate your negative behavior. If you give them everything, they will expect they are entitled to everything. Unless you have a never-ending bank account, then you're in trouble and so are they. Your children must know that the world is a difficult place and if you want your children to be responsible, you must prepare them for that reality.

What is the best method to discipline my child?

Sorry, you're on your own on this one. There is not a universal answer on disciplining a child. Each child is different and must be disciplined on an individual basis. One child may respond to a stern lecture, one may respond to sentence writing, or one may respond to a time-out. Only you can determine what the best way is through trial and error. Good luck!

Do I really need a good friend at this stage of my life?

If you are over two years old then you need a good friend. We learn from our friends from age two to age eighty. I still learn from my friends and I am proud to say they vary from their early 20's to late their 70's in age. I learn and seek their guidance daily. You are never alone as long as you have a friend.

Is it really important to be a "good" person? And is it important to be a "bad" person?

We all want to be good, but sometimes we just don't know how to pull it off. We must always attempt goodness and make it routine to do good in this world. This world has enough bad folks in it and we don't really need any additional bad.

FINAL THOUGHTS

I have spent many years on this good Earth. I have experienced many things and made more than a few mistakes along the way, I believe my mistakes and the lessons learned from them, can help others. I do not think sharing my lessons and mistakes will necessarily keep you from making the same mistakes, but there is a lot to be learned from what I have been through. I certainly do not have all the answers, but am not shy about offering my advice when asked. I try very hard not to offer any unwanted advice, and sometimes I fail at that, but at least I try! There are times when I almost think to myself "please ask me what I think" just so I can unload. It all boils down to having some thoughts, wanting to say them, but tempered with the cautionary. It's simple: *Don't Ask If You Don't Want To Know*.

I would love to hear from you so please feel free to reach out to me anytime at info@JeanieKnows.com with your questions, comments, or success stories.

Be sure to also visit my website JeanieKnows.com for more tips and ideas on having and maintaining healthy relationships in your life. And remember to smile every day!

ABOUT THE AUTHOR

Jeanie Frankavitz is a mentor and advisor to anyone who asks her to be. Born with the gift of being able to listen to people, she has spent her life sharing what she has learned with those who ask to hear her secrets to happiness and, at times, even to those who don't ask. Frankavitz is a child of the 1950's raised by parents of the World War II era, who were raised by the Great Depression era, so there was never a dull moment in her formative years. Harnessing all of her life experience, she is proud to be the loving Grandmother of five, mother of two, and wife of the most wonderful man in the world. She has traveled all over the US and currently lives in the Midwest. Always with a smile, Frankavitz shares much love for her fellow Earth dwellers.

FREE DOWNLOAD

Did you enjoy reading my book but have no idea how you plan on remembering everything you learned?

Would you like to have simple-to-use reminders to help you apply the tips and tools you learned from reading my book?

Do you want to stay connected with me so I can be that sassy voice of reason that helps you stay on track?

If you answered YES to any of the questions above, then be sure to download my free *Don't Ask If You Don't Want to Know* Daily Checklist Poster!

You can download my Daily Checklist Poster and print out as many copies as you need. Post them on your wall, desk, mirror, or anywhere else you know you'll see it on a daily basis for that constant reminder to *Clean Up Your Messy Life*.

CLAIM YOUR FREE DOWNLOAD AT:

www.JeanieKnows.com